Wayne Rooney

Mike Wilson

Published in association with The Basic Skills Agency

Hodder Murray

A MEMBER OF THE HO⋯⋯⋯P

The Publishers would like to thank the following for permission to reproduce copyright material:

Photo credits
p.2 © Matthew Peters/Man Utd via Getty Images; p.6 © Laurence Griffiths/Getty Images; p.10 © Matthew Ashton/Empics; p.13 © Mike Finn-Kelcey/Getty Images; p.19 © Scott Heavey/Rex Features; p.22 © Paul Webb/Rex Features; p.26 © Simon Bellis/ Reuters/Corbis.

Orders: please contact Bookpoint Ltd, 130 Milton Park, Abingdon, Oxon OX14 4SB. Telephone: (44) 01235 827720. Fax: (44) 01235 400454. Lines are open from 9.00–5.00, Monday to Saturday, with a 24-hour message answering service. Visit our website at www.hoddereducation.co.uk.

© Mike Wilson 2005
First published in 2005 by
Hodder Murray, a member of the Hodder Headline Group
338 Euston Road
London NW1 3BH

Impression number   10 9 8 7 6 5 4 3
Year   2010 2009 2008 2007 2006

Cover photo © Ian Hodgson/Reuters/Corbis
Typeset in 14pt Palatino by SX Composing DTP, Rayleigh, Essex.
Printed in Great Britain by CPI Bath.

A catalogue record for this title is available from the British Library

ISBN-10 0 340 90061 X
ISBN-13 978 0 340 90061 1

Contents

1 Chance of a Lifetime

In 1994, a young boy
went to Liverpool Football Club
for a football trial.
He was nine years old.

This trial was the chance of a lifetime.

If he did well, he might get a place
at Liverpool's Youth Academy.
The Academy was a school for young football talent.
Michael Owen, Stephen Gerrard
and Danny Murphy all started there.

The young boy had the chance to join Liverpool FC,
one of the biggest clubs in the country.

There was only one problem.

Wayne Rooney.

That problem was the shirt
the boy wore to the trial.

It was blue – an Everton shirt.
You don't go to play for Liverpool
in an Everton shirt.

Not unless you're Wayne Rooney.

Everyone could see
that nine-year-old Wayne Rooney
was going to be something special.

And everyone could see that
he was going to play for Everton,
not the local rivals Liverpool.

Not long after, Wayne got a call from Everton.
And there was no looking back.

2 Once a Blue, Always a Blue

Wayne Rooney was born on 24 October 1985.

His dad was a big Everton fan.
He got Wayne his first blue shirt
on the day he was born!

Wayne grew up a few miles
from Everton's ground, Goodison Park.

He was a good Catholic lad –
quiet, shy and polite.
He didn't shine at school subjects.
He didn't have a lot to say –
at least not until he got on the football field.

Wayne was football mad.
As soon as he started kicking a ball,
he started scoring goals.

Once, when he scored, Wayne lifted his shirt
to show the T-shirt underneath.
It read: *Once a Blue Always A Blue*!

Wayne was Everton mascot in 1996.
He had his photo taken
in the centre circle at Anfield
when Everton played Liverpool.

Then, when he was 12,
Wayne had his photo taken again –
with Everton striker Duncan Ferguson.

Years later, Wayne met Duncan Ferguson
for the second time.
It was a week after Wayne left school.
He was in the Everton first team squad
for a game at Southampton.

It was a dream come true.

He was 16 years old,
and he was in the same squad
as Duncan Ferguson, his Everton hero!

Wayne Rooney playing for Everton against
Birmingham City in 2002.

Even at that age,
there wasn't a weak side to his game.
Wayne was just as good with his left foot
as he was with his right.
He was big and strong, but fast as well.
He could leave defenders standing.

He was full of running.
He tackled hard and tracked back for the ball.
He could read the game
and make goals for his team mates.
He could run at defenders.

He could fire in unstoppable shots
from 30 yards (27.5 metres).
He could score from open play.
He could score from free-kicks
or diving headers.

And what about that cheeky shot
from the half-way line
that beat the Arsenal keeper?
Wayne didn't score, but he hit the bar!

Move over David Beckham!

3 Youth Team

Wayne signed up with Everton in December 2001.
He was 16 years old.
He was on the bench for some first team games.
He played in the Reserves and in the Youth Team.

Everton were bringing him on, slowly.
He was still a boy in a man's world.
They were introducing him, bit by bit,
to the life of a top professional footballer.

'I want to play in Everton's first team,'
Wayne said, 'because I've supported them
all my life.
But first team games are faster.
It's much more physical.
If I play too many games now,
I'll get injured in the long run.'

He seemed to have a wise head
on his 16-year-old shoulders.

Wayne could not get a game
in Everton's first team –
he was too busy playing for England!

Wayne scored five goals in five matches
in the UEFA Under 17s European Championship
in April and May 2002.
He got a hat-trick in the play-off against Spain.
England won 4–1, and took third place.

Back home, Wayne scored
eight goals in eight matches
in the FA Youth Cup in May 2002.
Everton got to the final,
but lost to Aston Villa.

It was all good training
for his call-up to Premiership football.

Wayne Rooney playing for England in the Under-17s
team in 2001.

4 First Team

Wayne was still waiting on the touchline
at the start of the 2001–2002 season.
It was still Everton's plan
to introduce their secret weapon bit by bit.

He came on as a sub in a few matches –
and he soon turned those games around.

His first game was against Wrexham
in the Worthington Cup.
Wayne came on in the second half.
He scored two goals in ten minutes,
helping Everton to a 3–0 win.

Wayne became the youngest Everton goal scorer.
He was still only 16!

Wayne will never forget his first goal
in the Premiership in October 2002.
It was against Arsenal,
and Arsenal hadn't been beaten for 30 games.

It was the last minute of the match.
Both sides seemed to have settled for a 0–0 draw.
Until Wayne blasted the ball in off the bar
from 25 yards (23 metres).

It was still a few days
before his seventeenth birthday.

In his next match – against Leeds –
Wayne did it again.
This time, he ran at the defence,
beat a couple of men
and scored from 10 yards (9 metres) out.

In his third Premiership match,
he scored one goal and set up another one:
Everton 2, Blackburn 1.

His next game was against Birmingham.
Wayne became the youngest player
in the Premiership to get a red card.
He still had a lot to learn!

Wayne Rooney getting a red card in the Everton v Birmingham City game in 2002.

By now, everyone was talking about Wayne Rooney.
In December 2002 he was voted
BBC Young Sports Personality of the Year.
People began to talk about
a £20 million price tag.

Wayne stayed calm, and said nothing.
He took it all in his stride.

Everton were still trying to protect him:
'He is not mature yet – on or off the pitch.'
said manager David Moyes.
'Ten years from now,
when Wayne is fit and strong,
and playing regularly for England,
he'll thank us for building him up slowly.'

But another manager didn't seem to think
Wayne needed building up slowly:
'Yes, he's only 17,' he said.
'But Pelé was 17 when he won the World Cup
in Sweden in 1958!'

That manager was the England manager
Sven-Göran Eriksson.

5 England

Wayne got his first full England cap
in February 2003.
He was 17 years and 111 days old.
That made him the youngest player
ever to play for his country.

The match was a disaster for England.
They lost 3–1 in a friendly with Australia.
Wayne came on at half-time,
when the whole team was changed.
Not even Wayne Rooney could turn the game around.
But it was all good experience.

Then, in September 2003,
England played Macedonia.
It was in the run-up to Euro 2004.
Wayne scored, and became the youngest player ever
to score for England.

The stage was set for Portugal – Euro 2004.

6 An Important Game

Meanwhile, back home,
Everton were doing well in the Premiership.
This was in the summer of 2003.
If they could finish the season in the top six,
they'd be in the UEFA Cup.

And they were in with a chance
– until the last game of the season.
Manchester United came to Goodison Park.
They had already won the Premiership,
so they didn't need the points.
But Everton needed to win,
so they could play in Europe next season.

It was not to be.
Manchester United won 2–1. Wayne failed to score.
He also got booked and picked up a knee injury.

Everton fans had good reason
to hate Manchester United that day!

7 Portugal

When Wayne went to Portugal
for the start of Euro 2004,
he was a regular in the England team.
By the end of the tournament,
he was England's hero.

In the first match against France,
England were 1–0 up by half-time.

Then, when Wayne was taken off,
England fell apart.
It took just two silly mistakes from England and
two flashes of genius from Zinedine Zidane.

France won 2–1.

England's hopes of a dream start were gone
in the last few seconds of the game.

England – and Wayne – did better
against Switzerland.
They won 3–0.
Wayne scored two goals and was Man of the Match.

The next match was against Croatia.
Wayne set up one goal and scored another
to put England ahead at half-time.
In the second half, everything came right
for England and Wayne Rooney.

Wayne worked a brilliant one-two
with Michael Owen on the half-way line.
The whole of the Croatian defence
was left standing.

With only the goalkeeper to beat,
Wayne looked right –
then slotted the ball to the left.
The keeper had no chance.

Wayne Rooney scoring his second goal against Croatia in Euro 2004.

Wayne looked cool and confident.
He'd scored four goals in three games
at international level.

England went on to win 4–2.
With Wayne playing like this,
England looked dangerous and strong.

But the next match was against Portugal.
Portugal had talent and flair.
They had Figo and Rui Costa, and Ronaldo.
They had strength in depth.

Yet after ten minutes, England were 1–0 up.
With his back to goal,
Michael Owen flicked the ball over the keeper
and into the empty net.
For the rest of the match,
England were fighting
to hold on to that slender lead.

Ten minutes later, disaster struck.

Wayne was fighting for the ball
with the Portuguese defender.
Wayne's boot came off.
A free-kick was given against him.

Wayne limped off the field.
He'd broken a bone in his foot –
the same bone David Beckham had broken
before the 2002 World Cup.

When Wayne left the pitch,
the spark went out of England's game.
They lost on penalties – as usual.

Wayne could only ask himself:
What if he'd still been on the pitch, at the end?
Would he have put his penalty
in the back of the net?
Could he have saved England?

Never mind. Wayne did all he could do.
He was England's hero – and top goal scorer.

And when he got back home,
everyone wanted Wayne Rooney!

Wayne Rooney limping off the field during the England v Portugal game, Euro 2004.

8 Once A Blue, Always A Red?

When Wayne got home from Portugal,
he had some thinking to do.

Sometimes he wished he could still
just hang around with his young mates.
Kick a football up against his gran's wall
like he did when he was a boy.
Be young, and do the things young boys do.
Be invisible.

But now he was famous all over the world.
He was recognised everywhere he went.

He had a brand new car, and a brand new house,
living near Sir Alex Ferguson.

Wayne had also got engaged
to his girlfriend Coleen.
He was growing up fast.

Everton manager David Moyes
knew what would happen next.
Other clubs would try to buy him.
'We don't want to lose Wayne
to another club,' he said.

'We think it's best for him
if he stays at Everton.
It's the club he's always supported.'

Everton offered Wayne £50,000 a week
to make him stay. Over five years,
the deal was worth over £12 million.
It wasn't enough.

In August 2004, Wayne joined Manchester United.
The deal was worth £30 million.
Everton got £10 million to start with.
The rest is linked to bonus targets
for years to come.

Everton supporters were let down.
Someone painted on the wall of Wayne's old house:
'You could have been an Angel.
But you chose to be a Red Devil.'

Wayne saw it differently.

'Over the last year,' he said,
'I have grown up a lot – on and off the pitch.
I've had to – a lot of people are trying
to bring me down.

'I know I can play at the top level,'
Wayne went on. 'Euro 2004 showed that.
But I need to be with a club
that plays in Europe every year.
I want to play in the Champions' League.

'Manchester United can give me that chance.
Everton can't.

'This has been the hardest decision of my life.
But I feel the time is right.
There will be more pressure.
But I know I'm big enough
and strong enough to handle it.'

Wayne Rooney scoring for Manchester United against Newcastle United in 2004.

Wayne's first match for United
was in September 2004.
It was in the Champions' League,
against Turkish champions Fenerbahce.

It was a dream start for Wayne.
He scored three goals –
all blistering shots from outside the box –
one with his left foot, one with his right,
and one free-kick.
Manchester United won 6–2.

Sir Alex Ferguson said Wayne was magnificent:
'The best young player we've seen in 30 years.'

So will Wayne Rooney bring European glory
back to Manchester?
Will he be England's hero for years to come?

Will Wayne be the new Paul Gascoigne . . .
the new David Beckham . . . or the new George Best . . .
or the new Pelé . . .?

Or will he simply be
the one and only Wayne Rooney?

9 Wayne Rooney Quiz

1 When was Wayne born?

2 How old was Wayne when he had a trial for Liverpool?

3 What did he do wrong at that trial?

4 What did it say on Wayne's T-shirt?

5 How old was Wayne when he first signed for Everton?

6 What was special about Wayne's first goal in the Premiership?

7 Who said that Wayne was like the young Pelé?

8 How many goals did Wayne score for England in Euro 2004?

9 Was he sent off in the match against Portugal?

10 Why did Wayne say he was leaving Everton?

11 How did Wayne do in his first match for Manchester United?

12 What is the name of Wayne's girlfriend?